THE GOSSAMER WALL

Micheal O'Siadhail was born in 1947. He was educated at Clongowes Wood College, Trinity College Dublin, and the University of Oslo. A full-time writer, he has published ten collections of poetry. He was awarded an Irish American Cultural Institute prize for poetry in 1982, and the Marten Toonder Prize for Literature in 1998. His poem suites, *The Naked Flame, Summerfest, Crosslight* and *Dublin Spring* were commissioned and set to music for performance and broadcasting.

His latest collections are *The Gossamer Wall* (Bloodaxe Books, 2002) and *Our Double Time* (Bloodaxe Books, 1998). *Hail! Madam Jazz: New and Selected Poems* (Bloodaxe Books, 1992) included selections from six of his collections, *The Leap Year* (1978), *Rungs of Time* (1980), *Belonging* (1982), *Springnight* (1983), *The Image Wheel* (1985), as well as the whole of *The Chosen Garden* (1990) and a new collection *The Middle Voice* (1992). A new selection of his earlier poetry, *Poems 1975-1995*, drawing on both *Hail! Madam Jazz* and his later collection *A Fragile City* (Bloodaxe Books, 1995), was published by Bloodaxe in 1999.

He has given poetry readings and broadcast extensively in Ireland, Britain, Europe, North America and Japan. In 1985 he was invited to give the Vernam Hull Lecture at Harvard and the Trumbull Lecture at Yale University. He represented Ireland at the Poetry Society's European Poetry Festival in London in 1981. He was writer-in-residence at the Yeats Summer School in 1991 and at the Frankfurt Bookfair in 1997.

He has been a lecturer at Trinity College Dublin and a professor at the Dublin Institute for Advanced Studies. Among his many academic works are *Learning Irish* (Yale University Press, 1988) and *Modern Irish* (Cambridge University Press, 1989). He was a member of the Arts Council of the Republic of Ireland (1988-93) and of the Advisory Committee on Cultural Relations (1989-97), a founder member of Aosdána (Academy of distinguished Irish artists) and a former editor of *Poetry Ireland Review*. He is the founding chairman of ILE (Ireland Literature Exchange), and was a judge for *The Irish Times* ESB 1998 Theatre Awards and the 1998 *Sunday Tribune*/Hennessy Cognac Literary Awards.

Micheal O'Siadhail's website: www.osiadhail.com

MICHEAL O'SIADHAIL

The Gossamer Wall

POEMS IN WITNESS TO THE HOLOCAUST

BLOODAXE BOOKS

ISBN: 1 85224 601 4

First published 2002 by
Bloodaxe Books Ltd,
Highgreen,
Tarset,
Northumberland NE48 1RP.

and simultaneously in the USA
by Time Being Books.

www.bloodaxebooks.com
For further information about Bloodaxe titles
please visit our website or write to
the above address for a catalogue.

Bloodaxe Books Ltd acknowledges
the financial assistance of Northern Arts.

Cover printing by J. Thomson Colour Printers Ltd, Glasgow.

Printed in Great Britain by
Cromwell Press Ltd, Trowbridge, Wiltshire.

For those who died,
for those who survived,
for those who told

A bite for me, a bite for you, an extra bite for Bella...
I felt her presence everywhere, in daylight, in rooms
I knew weren't empty...Watching with curiosity and
sympathy from her side of the gossamer wall.

ANNE MICHAELS, *Fugitive Pieces*

... the Devil is known to lure people into forgetting
precisely what is vital for them to remember....

ARTHUR MILLER, *The Crucible in History*

CONTENTS

Cataclysm

In each human moment as in the time of stone
Such build-up before a lava fumes in the cone.

Cumulative time, a gradual hidden crescendo,
Those lids of the earth's crust shifting below.

Rifts in a magma chamber, a vicious blow-up;
Bombs and cinders spewed from an angry cup.

Sleep Vesuvius that once covered up Pompeii
With pumice-stone and ash. Sleep and allay

What fears we must both remember and forget.
Sleep Vesuvius. Within us all your molten threat.

And yet. Another beginning. Another landscape.
Can the sun still sweeten even the sourest grape?

Shared scars of forgiveness, our fragile hopes;
The fruits and vines tended on your lower slopes.

LANDSCAPES

Vemen vil er gor gevinen?
Vos zaynen mir a flig?
Loz er undz a skhus gefinen.
Oy, es zol shoyn zayn genug!

What's He trying to put over?
What are we, flies in the wind?
Is there nothing in our favour?
Enough! It's got to end.

Song of the Balta Pogrom (1882)
translated by David G. Roskies and Hillel Schwartz

Numbers

1

As though the digit shifts of centuries
Disconnect what is from what has been,
Some magic in numbers seems to lure us
And wants to wipe our old slate clean,

Somehow to forget that it may well be
That on the shaft of its middle decade
(And not its end) the twentieth century
Turns, or to think those ghosts are laid

And can no longer remind us how
It's best another generation remembers
Never to forget it could happen now.
No, not so much to rake the embers

But to recall how something not faced
Goes underground and then reappears
To haunt us. An image of Iscariot traced
Wandering across two thousand years,

His embezzled silver, his turncoat kiss.
Deutschland erwache, Juda verrecke!
Two millennia blurring Jew and Judas;
Even in the betrayer's name an echo.

Beware, beware a beast that slumbers.
And so, both to remember and celebrate
A year turning on the axis of our numbers.
A new millennium. An ancient slate.

2

A half a century on, last camp survivors
Will still wear a number on their forearm;
A tremblor rippling fifty miles beyond
Its epicentre, patterning a garden pond.
Telltale figures, eerie signatures of violence.

In an aftermath the fortunate huddle together;
At least a marriage each day at Bergen-Belsen.
Obstinacy of survival, slowly reassembled life.
Why was I one of those chosen to survive?
For children, grandchildren? A demand to tell?

Masks of resilience gradually become a self;
Work and getting on against all the odds.
Always the long shadowed crux of that past:
Remember too much, the *Kapo* laughs last,
To forget breaks sacred promises to the gone.

Still the stamped forearms of first witnesses.
Indelible warnings: this might happen again.
Still a moment when testimony and story meet
Before the last attesting faces will retreat
To echo chambers of second-hand remembrance.

3

An intersection, at once cadence and overture,
Hinge and turning point, the moment when
The pasts we shape begin to shape our future.

Etty Hillesum recalled how her father had said
'Jews in a desert? We've seen the landscape before.'
Babylon, the Temple's fall, six million dead.

Give ear to my cry, don't hold your peace at my tears.
Is this the moment where testimony and story meet?
A passing guest, an alien like all my forebears.

Teach us, cries the psalmist, to number our days.
The exile, the scattering, now the ovens and marches.
Isaiah's world still stumbling onwards in praise.

Have I not told you from old you're my witnesses?
The desert through which we pass will bloom again.
I did not speak in secret in a land of darkness.

Remembrance

A word absorbed in an ease of childhood's garden
you think you've heard a million times over
suddenly will sink further in. A depth charge.

Or a piece you begin learning note by note,
slow practising by rote, a dreamlike repetition;
years go by before you re-awake to its music.

As though things can be too big for us close-up
and need the slow-down of both time and distance;
a wider angle, the gradual *adagio* of truth.

So complex, so tangled as if we have to wait
on some riff of imagination to refract detail,
some fiction to shape elusive meanings of fact.

Time to find the chronicles below the debris
of a cleansed ghetto, for piecemeal unearthings
to air their testimony against false witness.

Just quiet moves and shifts in geological tempo,
or the way climates show changes over decades
of slow landscape. A long redemption of time.

In a rest between notes a music's bridled silence
or in our fictions those things still best unsaid,
a tacit crying out for the forgiveness of the dead.

Forebodings

Rumbles in bowels of myth. Again and again
Eruptions, sulphurous gases of blame.
An inwoven scapegoat down two millenniums.

When Pilate had washed his hands: *See you to it.*
Then answered all the people and said
'His blood be on us and all our children'.

Scatterings. Ghetto. Yellow badge. Pogroms.
Who was it poisoned wells to spread
Black Death among Christian folk? *And they spit*

Upon him and took the reed and smote him
On the head. So Europe at fever pitch.
Crusades. Over again the Goyim's fall-guy.

Outsider inside. Love-hate's merry-go-round.
Blood-baker, healer, *Jude Süss.*
Even while the myth sleeps, a waiting victim.

Those angular planes overlapping and awry,
Tragic fault line within us,
Moody engines of prejudice underground.

Hankerings

Upheaval broods in the cauldron of an age.
Those thirty years of such faithful war –
Then Europe must struggle with her rage
For everything certain and hierarchical,
Three long centuries lusting after order.
Intolerance brews in her earth's mantle.

Rage for axioms, timeless abstractions:
Newton's laws, old Leibniz's universal;
Species, genus, our races and nations,
Europe hankers after all things steady.
A narrowing. A Renaissance in reversal.
A nervous urge to tame and already

We hunger for overviews, flawless stock,
Unblurred theories, the pure nightmare
Of ideal boundaries, *ein Land, ein Volk*.
Übermensch of dark-willed Nietzsche.
Outcastes, outsiders, freaks, beware
Our tick-tock reason's overreach.

What happened to Macbeth's carousing porter,
Montaigne's wry and carnival knowledge?
That marvelling at being just as we are,
Our lovely jumbled here-and-nowness,
Particular, once-off, centred at the edge,
This cussed and glorious human mess.

Lull

White noise and the chatter of foreshock
Along a fault; only the focus silent,
Some darker core of resentment.
Black shirts and polished boots,
Slogans of marchers with high-armed salutes.
Sultry Germany racked and knuckled under.
Tremblors wait in proud compressions of rock.

Versailles' humblings and rubbings-in;
Europe of boundaries settles bitter scores.
Too long a licking of sores
Rankles, a sour backlash
As after a first hard-won comeback the Crash
Of '29. So many half-hungry and idle.
Wounds fester under the earth's thin skin.

A wobbling trust. Dangerous subsoil.
At first too harsh, then a guilty placation.
Jutland, Somme, Verdun.
Thirty-five million.
And no, this could never happen again.
Seductive quiet. Sweet lulls of peace;
A seismic gap before a second turmoil.

Still yearnings for the glories of empires.
Dread of Bolsheviks. Upper crust and bourgeoisie
Longing for any certainty
Somehow appease and backslide.
Strut and vaunt of so much bruised pride.
All hail *Volk, Übermensch und Lebensraum!*
Let not light see my black and dark desires.

Spasm of precursors. Invisible shivers.
Lamentings heard i' th' air, strange screams of death.
In the sullen underneath
Slabs buckle in subduction
And prophesying with accents terrible of dire combustion.
Rock bends and strains towards its rupture.
A struck bell, the fabric of a planet quivers.

Reverberations

1

An old order to soldiers to lose their shape
As they march onto a bridge,
To break rhythm and march out of step

For fear concerted tempo might somehow match
Sways in the span and arch,
In case metered footfalls could catch

And amplify a beat to something vaster
Than just the sum of their paces;
A tapping into stone ripe for disaster.

2

After Napoleon the western ghetto
Vanishes. New epoch of citizenship,
Their loyalties now to flag and nation,
Rights, adaptations, *aggiornamento.*

But in vasts of White Russia, Poland,
Ukraine, Lithuania, Yiddish enclaves;
Always an outcast to Orthodox Slavs,
Catholic Poles, Lutheran *Volksdeutsch.*

Gulfs of language, religion and scorn.
Europe of nationhoods and borders,
Older jaundices, seething mistrusts;
The enclaved with nowhere now to turn.

Troop-carriers rumble over bridges:
Oder, Vista and Bug to a landscape
Already ashiver with deep grudges,
Bitter resonance of creaking divides.

Stress and strains of broken history
Prime a ruthless moment. A reverberation
Unleashes rage, a vicious licence
For minor Macbeths and *Übermenschen.*

In a sweep between Baltic and Black Sea
The Reich's own and echoed fury;
Chiming hatred, a boosted violence,
An ashen zone on Europe's hazard map.

3

Wavers on a seismogram, a wider scribble,
Shifts and jostlings along a seam until
The moment mother earth bucks and quavers.

Violence spreads out on every side,
Frenzy of pulses radiates and woe betide
A jellied soil, any sympathetic ground

That dances to its rhythms. Shocks caught
And magnified. Even worse havoc wrought
Far from the epicentre. Consonance of terror.

Wilderness

How on the Day of Atonement Aaron came
In linen garments to choose by lots
For the Lord one of two goats
And the other, sin-bearer for the Children of Israel,
He drove, a scapegoat into the wilderness.

Assimilated. Established. Even heroes of the Fatherland.
Liver of blaspheming Jew,
Gall of goat and slips of yew...
Once more the butt of every simmering prejudice
For th'ingredience of our cauldron.

Mischief bubbles. Strange conjunction of forces,
Hoarded pressures under duress,
Whatever slow or insidious process
Belches from its maw pent resentments
Through old hidden rifts and fissures.

In neighbouring shadows of politburos and commissars
The manufacturer, the entrepreneur
Still seem threatened and insecure;
Blond and blue-eyed redeemers of lost territory
Askance at swarthy interlopers.

Cornered every way. Marx the Jew boy,
Arch-Bolshevik, ogre and bane
Of commerce or just non-Aryan
Sallow-skinned, jet-haired rogue insider,
Hinge and axis of German shame.

Or is it some scheming international Rothschild,
A plot of dangerous infidel,
Shylock way out of scale,
Sly, alien, worldwide tissue of collusion
Menacing a stooped and brittle *Volk*?

Whatever the angle, same kinetics of mistrust.
Sweet incense beaten small
And bring it inside the veil.
O Aaron so unsuspecting in your linens of atonement.
Target of all. Our consummate scapegoat.

Signatures

1

Freylekh, Bulgars, waltzes and Klezmorim
Playing with such a confused abandon
Dances at once rumbustious and sad that seem

To summon up centuries of teeming ghetto life,
Weddings, bar mitzvahs, circumcision feasts
Hoisted out of the ordinary into some repetitive

Delight in sound – almost like those *céilí*
Bands melodeoning out their tunes
Battered and entrancing, a kind of cyclical gaiety

That goes on gathering its own quickened logic
Of unbroken desire. Or do they recall
Zigzag tensions and rhythms of Gypsy music?

And suddenly you hear the raucous joy of a trumpet,
A Black cotton-picker's reveille
Against the blues line of a wandering clarinet.

Then a Yiddish alto: 'There is my resting place'
Dorden ist mayn rue platz.
Each of these millions, someone's remembered face.

2

Surely all tragedies are both singular and one;
Those arcs of island over our human fault zone.

An uncouth and ruthless Georgian's litany of woe.
Ten million scorch-earth kulaks.
Purges and riddances. The Gulag archipelago.

Hatches battened on a reek of fevered steerage
Skibbereen to Grosse Isle
Ghosts of famine cross on their ragged voyage.

Some of their ships had once cargoed slaves,
Sugar drones and cotton-pickers,
The northern cities' Black slums and enclaves.

Middle passage of the dispossessed. Long transit
Of coffin-ships and camp trains,
Gangways and stations where their shades meet.

Hidden signatures of pain in a planet's hearth.
Quakes and eruptions linked in the underearth.

3

And yet there's no Richter scale of tragedy.
How to measure suffering? A calculus of pain?
Behind each agony a name, a voice, a face.

A quarter million Gypsies, the gays, the insane,
Soviet prisoners of war. The Slavs would be
Hewers and drawers under the master race.

But an unhinged and single-minded bid to erase
Every man, woman, child? Police and bureaucrat,
All will connive. There'll be no resting place.

Factories, trains and railroads now gearing up,
Machinery of oiled governance in a modern state;
Grindings and cogs of greasy calculation

And the one strain singled out for elimination.
This breed apart. A whole apparatus of hate
Bent on wiping a people from Europe's face.

Entrance

1

Convulsions in mother earth, the trembling rock;
Blind forces, a chronology of fault segments.

Ground swell of history, compulsions of an epoch;
Part of, tied into, caught up in grand events.

Marionettes? And yet decisions made, the ties,
The hitches, the twists which ravel us into a plot

Too intricate to comprehend. The eye tries
To follow its loops but strays in baffles of a knot.

Implications of grand doings and small choices.
Both bound up and binding. A complex ligature

Shaping this history that's also shaping us.
Could there be a Desolation without *der Führer*?

2

Enter the Austrian, history's fevered catalyst.
Vaulting ambition, which o'erleaps itself:
Shy, artistic and would-be watercolourist.

Volunteer artillery spotter, brave courier,
Three times wounded, twice an Iron Cross;
Now discharged corporal, disgruntled gurrier.

A somnambular voice invokes a latent anger,
His eyes singling out yours among the crowd.
Sleek-headed Chaplin. Mesmeric hate-monger.

Human, we want to explain away the villain.
Remember him only for the number of his victims.
Human? Is something already drawing us in?

3

And how to contain this unbearable evil?
Grails of theory, myths of explanation
Struggle to pin down one psychic upheaval

To make a make-up more easily understood.
Skeletons rattle in the ogre's cupboard,
A spirit tainted by a stain of Semite blood?

Grandmother Schicklgruber's seedy blackmail?
One-ball thesis? An apocryphal Jewess?
Strivings to bring a monster down to scale.

Part compassion, a *there-but-for-fortune*
Instinct stretches itself to analyse
Primrose paths, to understate the demon.

Part consolation, craving for simple clear-cut
Formulas, somehow to tame the untameable,
Undo inexplicable tangles of this blackest knot.

4

A bottomless puzzle. No matter how we rummage
So much eludes us,
So much remains hidden
In shimmies and connivances, a stage-managed image.

Clearance to Madagascar that will slide even further
On highs of a Russian invasion,
A gradual Final Solution?
Or from the start intent on some bureaucracy of murder?

Poisonous ideologue, deluded purger of Jewry,
Half-possessed messianic?
A cunning manipulator
Scheming determinedly in a cold-blooded fury?

Or both? At first a cynic's deceiving art,
The gestures, the counterfeit;
As the crowds feedback belief
A bestriding actor overcome by his own part.

Hungary, Poland, Czechoslovakia, the Ukraine,
Headiness of triumph, hubris,
Believing his own image.
Till Birnam forest come to Dunsinane.

Unwholesome radiance. A devious implacable will
Outpaces all explanation.
The black sun shines.
Quantum leap in some darker mystery of evil.

Signals

Electrical changes, rumours of foreshock,
Hints and tremolos sensed by animals
Tuning in to some seismic signals;
A dog yelps and chickens jitter.

Can no one hear the yearning oracle?

Heine's premonishing a century in advance,
A forlorn Cassandra
Warns the *Heimat* from exile in France.

A Munich newspaper's near-daily reports
Of fatal beatings,
By gangs of thugs and party cohorts,

Break-ins, demimonde of counter extortion,
Dirt on rivals,
Nexus of blackmail and poison pen.

Editor Gerlich will be lifted by the Gestapo,
Steel-rimmed blood-spattered
Glasses returned to a soon-to-be widow.

An English civil servant writes to London:
The Jew is to be eliminated –
A cold intelligence is planning in Berlin

The fate of a kulak or a Turkish Armenian –
And the State has
No regard for the manner of his elimination.

Processions to Britain of opposition emissaries,
Coolly rebuffed
Suspect double-crossers in Europe of boundaries.

Strange vibes and currents in rocks
Reptile sense before earthquakes;
In hoar-frost the hibernating snakes
Stir from a warm underground lair.

Will no one see when the serpent rises?

Vignettes

1

'I was with A.H.', his secretary will remember,
'When he arrested Röhm and the SS chiefs.'
The last hours of June 1934
At Bad Weisee. Night of the Long Knives.

Brownshirt leaders, outliving their usefulness,
Barracked overnight for morning executions.
'Back at the Chancery canteen,' she recalls,
'He'd joined me (both of us were vegetarians)

'But left for an hour, then called from the door:
So Fräulein Schröder, now I've had a bath,
I'm pure as a new-born babe once more'.
Relished moments. That knowing laugh.

2

Bathhouse there? A cleansing furnace?
Architects pore over detailed drafts.
Steps to chambers and then ramps.
Someone's busy working on an elevation.
The space where trains can pull in,
Perhaps a selection area just here?

And there'll be the minutiae: a pipeline,
Conduits, switches, the width of vents,
Probably a time and motion study
To check smooth running of machinery.
But for now, just a sense of proportion,
All focus still on the overall design.

Aesthetic of function. Delicate efficacy.
The tall pleasing line of a chimney,
A low contour of a kitchen and laundry.
Gate motto: ARBEIT MACHT FREI.
Work makes you free. Arch-joke
For connoisseurs. Malign surrealism.

3

Underground. Eastern Front command post.
Midnight tea and cakes. At two mein host
Grows expansive, holding forth until dawn.

Table talks. Monologues. *Der Führer* oracular
As a secretary shorthands each thought for posterity;
Art, philosophy, literature, the state of the war.

Tonight's guests Heydrich and Himmler. *Macbeth
Does murder sleep.* Trio of would-be virtuosi:
The watercolourist, violinist, architect of death.

Gradual bonds of complicity, a 'blood-cement'.
And no written orders just a word to the wise
Making its way down to middle management.

Needless violence of the camps. Yes, gratuitous
And yet somehow even more a painstaking
Theatre of malice, *ars gratia artis.*

Extermination? 'Silly,' he says, 'A silly rumour,
We simply park our Jews in the Russian marshes.'
A nod and wink. *Der Führer* in high good humour.

*From this instant, there's nothing serious in mortality.
All is but toys.* A play of nudges for the gallery.
An ironic distance. Three great artists of evil.

Brink

Shelves of the earth shunt on different levels;
Forces of conflict
Climax in violence.
But this human tangle of evil almost unravels;
A turn of events,
One sudden twist,
A bitter history's last minute head-over-heels.

His vote now fallen, a waning star,
Der Führer holds a splintering party
With veiled threats of self-murder.

Hindenburg, tottering junker president
About-faces. A backstairs deal turns
'That Austrian corporal' to 'dear young friend'

And haughty Papen thinks he'll rein in
The beast and can not see *Tarquin's
Ravishing strides towards his design.*

Tainted by the Night of Long Knives,
A first smear of the blood-cement,
Soon the arrogant Reichswehr connives.

A fractious left in one-eyed disorder
Squanders their last chance majority,
Too busy settling some old score.

'A miracle', *der Führer* calls his success.
Thousands torch-light Wilhelm Straße.
The opposition slips away into darkness

As entering his office the new Chancellor
Confides to someone in his entourage:
'Nothing will dislodge me alive from here.'

How nearly it didn't happen. Fortune's somersault,
Blind worm of disaster,
A blundering drama,
Tragedy of this black knot somehow tied by default.
Sophocles watches.
The flaw. The downfall.
So little might have brought a juggernaut to a halt.

DESCENT

S'brent! briderlekh, s'brent!
Oy, undzer orem shtetl nebekh brent...!
Un ir shteyt un kukt azoy zikh
Mit farleygte hent...

Fire, brothers, fire!
Our poor town's on fire...!
While you stand there looking on
With folded hand...

Mordeccai Gebirtig
translated by David G. Roskies

Northeim

Heimat

Thirty-one-year-old and tanned Wilhelm Spannaus
peers out of a rundown train window
on his return from seven years in South America.

1921, after a rising in the Rhineland
none of the glory of the Wilhelmine Reich
he'd left. Is the fatherland to be a Marxist shambles?

A brother had fought and perished in the world war.
Another in academe. Wilhelm will run
his father's bookshop, the first one ever in town.

Scion of old burghers and his father's gentlest son,
friendly with everyone, soon he'll be
intellectual drum and energy for his midland city.

Staunch Lutheran, acquaintance of poets and thinkers
he'll fan the embers of recalled glory
to become the first of the Party members in the burgh.

There's a distrust of visionaries, and rumours abound
of thugs and power-lust but people will say
Wilhelm Spannaus is involved, it must be in order.

To tidy things up. To revive a lustrous German soul.
Every pane is broken in the whole rumbling
train that snakes across the heartland into Northeim.

Northeim

In the fallout of defeat a city of ten thousand
nooked where the Leine and Ruhme meet,
this snug county seat plump in the heartland
rides the slump as a thousand other towns
where a seventh of Weimar Germany resides.

A cloister under Charlemagne, a Guelph city,
self-driven Hanseatics, then Lutherans
besieged and riven in the Thirty Years War.
Merchants surrender but the have-nots resist.
A broken power with its relics of old splendour,

Steep-roofed, small-paned jumble of houses
with timber designs; a medieval wall
defines a core of narrow cobbled streets.
Centuries of a comeback: a market and garrison
town become a pivotal midland junction.

Spur-lines, goods yards and a sugar refinery,
as commerce expands towards the Leine,
a retinue of railroad hands, tradesmen,
artisans, government clerks, teachers, newcomers
freighting Marx's credo to a rifting Northeim.

Beyond the wall a bourgeoisie northward
Toward the Ruhme, on a hill to the south
the wealthy nest as the lower ranks spill
west to the railroad hub; a cleft geography
soon mirrored in every beer-club and choir.

Two hundred and fifty three Northeimers dead
in Wilhelm's war. An inbred love
of marching is fed by fife and drum bands,
a complaisant town rife with slogans, banners,
and a military zest still not chastened by history.

Desires and ruptures no one will heed in time.
Self-betraying Northeim, a burgh still
smug in its divides until under pressure
of Nazi assault its wedged boundaries sunder
along an old fault line. A fissured city.

Kingpin

Ernst Girmann, the Party dynamo, an angry
Twenty-six-year-old son of a Northeim incomer
Hardware merchant, cool, grey-eyed and hungry.

Like his *Führer*, an Iron Cross from World War One
Where a brother fell. But whatever died within,
Here's a man ruthless, consumed by ambition,

His dark blond hair split precisely mid-skull
And sleeked to the sides, thin lips and cleft chin,
A young ruddy face too knowing and vengeful.

An engine of upheaval. Every ruse and stratagem.
Short-fused and underhand; when drunk maudlin,
He despises Northeim for years they ignore him.

An endless programme of unrest until the city's
Fissures gape and the group leader can begin
To weed his rivals out, to purge committees.

The Bürgermeister ousted, opponents collapse
As Girmann seizes power, local kingpin
In a regional gridiron of smaller Party satraps.

Once in control, a round of graft and patronage,
Resentments against an aloof elite, driven
By chips and grudges of *petit bourgeois* umbrage.

Vendettas. Anyone who'd crossed his path before.
The former city manager flees to save his skin.
A usurper's long memory for any unsettled score.

Failure to suppress the once supportive Lutherans
Galls him. He learns the tyrant's oldest chagrin:
To settle for the half-cheek of ritual obeisance.

As the Americans approach, his final orders are
To defend the city to the death. Unfrocked Girmann
Loads his *Schnapps,* decamps for the hills by car.

Three years interned and he'll settle in a town close
To Northeim. Later some stubborn tug of origin
Will return to its own an ageing and sullen recluse.

Fever Chart

Suddenly a fringe of zealots in from the cold.
The panache to hold a town at fever pitch.
Flags, a flash of black on white on red,
torch-light parades, blurted radio speeches,
children wearing swastikas, vertigo of elections,
rumours of the Gestapo, fracas, stormtroopers,
book burnings, cheering rallies, brass bands.

Suddenly a fringe of zealots move mid-stage.
Speakers planned to engage a middle class.
'Only one God in heaven we love, one fatherland,'
A Lutheran priest exhorts a crowd who applaud
rapturously. Girmann and cohorts tack and trim
to meet demands; self-tuned feedback of success,
a balance sheet of members, dues and votes.

Suddenly a fringe of zealots centre of attention.
Funded from the ground up, tactics hinge
on the leader's flair to sound the local mood;
once the coffers fill, the Gauleiter doesn't care.
To elude a backlash, Girmann soft-pedals Jews
but stokes every feud and panic in a riven city.
One clear-cut goal: the *realpolitik* of power.

Suddenly a fringe of zealots into the limelight.
Fuzzy talk of kin and forebears and blood
but there's an élan, a vehemence about the men,
a sense of purpose that seems to promise some
new ordinance, a millennium on earth. Farmers'
sons from Northeim County swell the marches
as old dreams well in the citizens' giddy hearts.

Suddenly a fringe of zealots in from the wings.
To keep things on the boil until the burghers
tire of all this turmoil and rancour and begin
to hanker again after the fist of certainty.
Anything for order. Riots dismissed as a phase,
the crowd cheer, sing the Horst Wessel Song.
A dizzying city skitters along the brink.

Butt

In fevers of stoked upheaval
How come the decent won't stand as one
Or somehow see behind the show and pageantry
Sleight-of hand, a jugglery of evil?
But none
So blind as those who will not see.

A left wing lose their way.
No bridges to the middle, their dreams
Of sweeping change a rhetoric out of touch;
Shadow marches, the *Internationale,*
And schemes
For a counter-coup, a phantom putsch.

Imagining themselves bereft
Of wealth and power, the Bourgeoisie
Hatch fears of a shake-up. A need to condemn
The *bête noire* of an upstart left
Won't see
The beast they feed will feed on them.

Communists gloat: at least
The spineless left is dealt a blow!
Guelphs still fight the ghosts of a lost cause,
Both fall prey to the hungry beast
And so
A town succumbs to tragic flaws,

Feckless squabbles, disunities.
A Blackshirt machine adjusts or shifts,
The thinner end and then the blunter edge,
A *coup d'état* by stealth, as a city's
Rifts
Widen to the bullying butt of a wedge.

Wilhelm

The Party digs in. A legerdemain of office.
Graft. Gravy train. Shuffles of embezzlement.

In Spannaus' bookshop mumbled dissent.
Was this the dream they meant to espouse?

Corruption could only undermine *das Volk*,
they grumble up the line to the Gauleiter

And no one listens. Girmann sews it up.
The black sun shines in blacker satellites.

Teacher friends hounded, Spannaus clings
to belief: *der Führer* would clean things up.

Wide-eyed trust. And many in town still say:
if Wilhelm is involved, it must be in order.

Power

1

A sudden caller to Schulenburg throws
a Swastika pin on his table: Put that on
or else! The aloof county prefect caves in.

An eye to preferment, civil servants join.
Spouse cajoles spouse, for our sake apply.
Rumbling momentum as a bandwagon rolls.

A tavern installs a radio to tout *der Führer*'s
speeches; Girmann's blunt brother puts out
signs on a shop-front: First Member in County.

A party of some hundred paid up the January
before. Now a scramble to become a member.
By December a fifth of Northeim's adults enlist.

Baskets of requests. The *Gruppenführer* sneers
at how after years fair-weather friends convert
and rubs his old opponents' noses in the dirt.

Some who oppose him enroll, want to give
the whole a leaven of decency, some dither
watching to see just how the wind blows.

The despised appeasers. Once in, no leaving.
Once compromised and in, the squeezers on,
A marked man while the black sun shone.

2

It spread by rumour
That one evening at a party in the town
Ruhmann the doctor, after a drink or two
Had let his hair down
And did his take-off of *der Führer*.

Next morning his hostess
Reports his behaviour for fear it may redound
On her that the doctor had done his party-piece.
The word gets round
Better not to party just in case.

Better to stay
At home. Clubs they'd once joined
Have been rearranged or merged 'to aid cohesion'.
What's the point
When you watch every word you say?

Nothing too clear.
Talk of blacklists no one lays eyes on.
Everybody wonders who the moles are, everybody
Warns someone;
Shadow efficacy of hearsay and fear.

A few disappear
Enemies cold-shouldered and driven out.
A news photo of a camp some hours away
That's whispered about,
Vague menaces in the atmosphere.

Enough just
For numb compliance. Terror seems to travel
And amplify like a myth as frail bonds of friendship
Begin to unravel.
Tacit threats. Meltdown of trust.

3

Now to warrant Girmann's iron hand
grand schemes to smarten Northeim
and prime a pump of Nazi upsurge.
A splurge of paint on medieval buildings.
Things on the move, a massive overhaul.
The wall around the town repaired,
an uncared for chain of defence mounds
that surrounds the city landscaped to create
ornate parks or gardens and the one-time
Northeim moat becomes instead a ring

of flattering lakes for swans. Everywhere
an air of purpose. A brand new
venue The Sacred Place (which stood
in a wood of tall oaks a henchman
of Girmann sold for a favourable sum),
a stadium which lures tourists to town.
Rundown areas cleared and re-planned,
demand for uniforms heartens business,
an address by Girmann to entrepreneurs
avers the end of the slump is in reach
if each of them employs more. Spend,
lend or borrow, above all consume.
Boomtown in the making. A house scheme
the regime they'd ousted tried they now
allow, though they stymied it before.
More public works. The Shirts know
how a show of action will for a while
beguile the burghers. Lulled for a time,
Northeim believes what Northeim desires.

Them

Girmann had threatened to expel some members
for hobnobbing with them. As the Reich began
to settle, a determined plan to freeze them out.

A haberdashery that a year before toasted two
hundred and thirty years. A grocery store.
A draper. A broker. Six score in ten thousand.

A newspaper names every store and office
to boycott. Few Northeimers dare to ignore
the SA man posted at the door of a premises.

A chance to capitalise on not to be missed.
A sign: GERMAN MERCHANT now vies with:
PURELY CHRISTIAN FAMILY ENTERPRISE

No one credited the rhetoric before the Reich;
now from fear neighbours start to shun them.
Their slide to isolation has already begun.

A burgher urged by another to flee shrugged:
'*Verstehen Sie*, here I'm Müller the Banker,
anywhere else I'd only be Müller the Jew.

A discreet push from a Veterans' Shooting Club
and Ballin the doctor crosses over the street
so as not to greet and taint his gentile friends.

A Shirt on his door, Ballin crumples. Numb
to the core, he keeps repeating: Was it for this
I spent four years to defend my fatherland?

Friends, colleagues, clients that shied away.
Slow isolation. Unprimrosed slide to a hell.
Blind-eyed Northeim doesn't want to know.

Stand-off

Northeim's *Geist* dumbed
Down to passivity. Numbed
And shrunken. What could you do?
Who would you trust or turn to?

As the Reich settles in
The once mirage of a genuine
Millennium fades. Disillusion.
Apathy. Denial. Accommodation.

A pretended daily compliance,
A sort of determined indifference
Where no one quite knew
Who was fooling who?

A need to keep the facade,
A zealous mutual charade:
The town dresses its window,
The Party approves the show.

An agreed unspoken stand-off.
Secretly many now scoff
At a dull regime; small
Comforts of inward withdrawal

That achieve nothing to halt
The iniquity. A spirit stalled,
A willed and grievous oblivion
While the black sun shone.

Huff-no-move of acquiescence.
Soft collusions of silence.

Battalion 101

Point-blank

Blueprint for a cleansed Europe. *Judenfrei.*
March '42 to February '43
at least three quarters of all the butchery.

Timetablers, a retinue of paper Rommels
shunt millions until there's only a residue,
a last few rump-ghettos and labour camps.

Feats of planning. Meticulous follow through.
But who rounded them up in scattered villages
sealed the trains or slew the lame and frail?

Everyday men. The plain and run-of-the mill
as Battalion 101 whose rank and file
would shy at first from point-blank slaughter.

Truckers, stevedores from Hamburg's docklands,
waiters, factory hands, clerks and small-time
salesmen; an average trawl of average citizens.

A mean of thirty-nine, too old for soldiers,
but drafted as *Ordnungspolizei* to clean up
Poland between the River Wisła and the Bug.

Men long grown before the black sun shone
from a city well-known for ease with outsiders.
Peer conformity, some bone-bred deference

Or any war's need to annul the victim's face?
Humdrum murder, dull and commonplace
as weeks lull them into a norm of violence.

Resettlements. Proceed as usual. Smoothly
again without incidents. Immunities of routine.
Ordinary men hardening in their daily carnage.

A Polish Village

1 *Débutants*

After the onslaught in Russia they know
a tour there left their men distraught
but in June when a mainline to Sobibór
was under repair Globocnik had soon
started to prepare for more shootings.
Under his care in Poland there's still
almost two million to kill and though
he'll use Treblinka and Bełżek, to slow
now would lose momentum. Clearly
slaughter is troublesome for men, yet
just then a war dangles in the balance
and summer is a chance he can't miss.
For want of better, the firing squads
of débutant Battalion 101.

2 *Rumour*

A few had guarded the sealed wagons
of Jews and Gypsies eastward, knew
from what they piece together better
not to wait and the escort commander
Gnade decided on the late train
and fled straight back to Hamburg.
A police battalion still unblooded.
July 12th when, less one company
they mass, a few had begun to wonder
if this meant their cue for *Judenaktion*.
The one dissident platoon commander,
a Hamburg timber merchant warns
his battalion commander's adjutant
he won't do it; as officer or merchant
he can't gun down bereft women
or infants. Unknown to his captain he left
to escort the 'work Jews' to Lublin.
A sergeant's caution to any who'd shirk:
he wants no cowards among his men.

Captain Wohlauf of First Company
Tips some off to next day's interesting
projects. Spare ammunition and whips
distributed. Everywhere there's rumour.

3 *Aside*

Roused early, some few are aware
what's ahead for them at Józefów
as trucks loaded with reserve bullets
jounce and swerve the dawning road
east to pounce on a sleeping village.
A weeping commander starts to speak
of a terrible task. A bleak assignment.
But after all orders are orders and
remember in Germany bombs fall
on both women and small children.
The Jews' American boycott harmed
the Fatherland. Armed partisans among
the three thousand eight hundred Jews
in Józefów just had to be kept in hand.
Fit men apart, the residue of women,
children and frail must now be shot
on the spot. Any who shied from the task,
should please immediately step aside.
One. Then, a dozen more will seize
this last chance before the massacre.

4 *Lesson*

Company platoons surround the village.
Fugitives are shot. The others round
them up in the market. Anyone gives
trouble, gun them with infants or feeble
or any who hide. Able-bodied men
set aside for camps as 'work Jews'.
The rest shuttled from the market place
to a nearby forest and the firing squads.
A swift session in how best to kill.

The battalion doctor (a gifted piano
accordionist at soirées) in order to show
the ways you ensure an instant release
depicts the contour of a human head
and shoulders, shows a fixed bayonet
set on the backbone above the blades.
Freighted forty at a time to the woods,
victims climb down to be assigned
a policeman each, lined up and pressed
to sites in the forest Wohlauf chose
and made now to lie in rows, a bayonet
as prescribed above each shoulder blade.
The sound of a first fusillade. Work-Jews
Throw themselves on the ground and weep.

5 *Haste*

Wohlauf all day keeps on the go
choosing sites so the incoming batch
won't see corpses. Two squads despatch
truckloads in relays. A messy business.
A blundered aim and blood sprays
anywhere. Splinters of sundered skulls.
The flurried officers begin to despair.
Men from the market are brought in.
Everyone ought to shoot. Hurried
changes to the process: a two–man escort
to the sites for speed. A few who ask
are sent to a different task, but Wohlauf
refuses his men any other assignment:
'If you can't take it, then lie down
with all the Jews.' A cigarette break.
In the afternoon, alcohol for the squads
as more approach their platoon leader
to be excused from the gore. Some shun
the shootings, others after one ordeal
on a pretext will dodge or steal away.
Some just delay the action. The evening
of a long summer's day and a feverish
drive to finish; as darkness falls

none will survive. Reloaded trucks
head west into the night, leaving
a strewn and looted dead behind.

6 *Nightmare*

Back at the barracks horror sinks in.
Dismayed or angry they begin to drink.
Oblivion of the bitter and afraid. Again
Trapp will calm his men, tell them
others are accountable. Orders are orders.
Best not to dwell on it. But those not
in the forest will neither ask nor pry
and those who were will try to forget.
Suppressed despair. Józefów
a taboo by consensus and self-excuse.
Jews were doomed no matter what,
so one more shot counted for little.
Not everybody can yet execute infants,
but one could only shoot the youngest
as he just can't bear to leave an orphan.
Some men declare they'd go mad
if they ever had to do the like again.
One wakes the night after Józefów
riddling a barracks roof with bullets.

Papa Trapp

Iron Crossed veteran of World War One,
at fifty-three a career policeman risen
through the ranks with his *esprit de corps*
but short on the blinder zeal of two captains
Wohlauf and Hoffmann who can't now conceal
young, arrogant contempt for their commander.
Yet Papa Trapp is popular among his men.

God, why did I have to be given these orders?
That day at Józefów he'd cry for the bloodshed;
aloof and riven he'd paced his headquarters
but not the forest. Things commanded not faced.
In despair he'd shed tears and confided to one
of his men *If ever this Jewish affair is avenged
on earth, then have mercy on us Germans.*

As the police reboarded trucks at Józefów
a ten-year-old girl bleeding from the head
appeared, he took her in his arms and said
You shall remain alive. Horror-struck
he'll console troops, overlook the truancy
of men who stole away or stepped aside.
Patron of all who flinch. A major who wept.

Come September a sergeant slain by ambush
and Lublin demands a minimum two hundred
punishment shootings to subdue locals. Trapp
still balks at Poles but with a mayor's consent
he'll kill just down-and-outs; instead the Jews
from a nearby ghetto can overfill his quota.
And Papa Trapp has no more tears to shed.

Measures

Apart from the merchant who first stepped aside
Or a dozen more who took a stand,
The trouble is the new recruits are horrified
By slaughter at first hand.
Squalor and gore are a burden,
Such distress could well unhinge their men.

True, a mind gets used to almost anything.
But a conscript tailor on a second relay,
Given a German mother and daughter for gunning
Sought release from the fray,
Returned to the market place.
The trouble is these killings face to face.

A merchant encountered among the men
In the market a Hamburg Jew;
Another's first job a war veteran from Bremen
Who'd begged in vain for rescue.
Morale will only improve
If the dirty work is kept at one remove.

Yet once posted to Lublin District everything
Seems at least more bearable.
Treblinka's death engine is in full swing.
A blind eye turned to hell,
Trapp's *Ordnungspolizei*
Elude the horrors of seeing how victims die.

Still violent round-ups. *Schnell! Schnell!*
Poke and herd. The murdered slow
Or fragile, the sweated driven pell-mell
Of parched human cargo
Nailed in a cattle wagon,
A freight of Jewry penned and shunted on.

Ukrainian, Latvian, Lithuanian underfed
War prisoners, the dreaded *Hiwis*,
Move in if there's any more bloodshed.
Measures taken to ease
The burden. A system refined.
A butchery out of sight and out of mind.

Lieutenant Gnade

A few courageous dissidents,
some who tend to skulk but take no stance,
the bulk of ordinary men who toe a line
of slow inurement;
in others a beast awakens.

Hartwig Gnade, Lieutenant
Mercy, who only eight months ago went
by late train back from Minsk so not to know
his cargo's fate
now turns cruel and violent.

As they dig their hole he'd choose
twenty greybeards to undress, and to amuse
himself compels them to crawl before their grave,
yells at his officers
to club these naked Jews.

Wobbling and enraged he'll sit
on a mound above the trench firing on it;
as teeming bodies shove into this tumulus
he's screaming drunken
abuse from the edge of the pit.

And in the colder late autumn
he'll institute his strip-search for every victim
to loot valuables. Returned their underwear,
they leave en route
for Treblinka shamed and numb.

Surges of a deep and molten
fury vie with *Hiwis* for cruelty; sudden
vicious shifts of humour terrify even
his men. An anger
amok. Vesuvius within.

Hoffmann

Another bred in a youth movement,
a touchy and headstrong twenty-year-old
ten years in the SS, then captain of a company,
a careerist who loves to parade his full insignia,
his white gloves and whose men dub him
'Hitler's cub scout'.

At Józefów when the timber merchant
withdrew and one of Captain Hoffmann's men
was among the few who dared to follow suit
he openly abused his recruit for breaking ranks
but Trapp excused the man and reined
his captain in.

Until October Company Three
Still eluded the worst. (At Józefów
they hadn't seen the shootings at first hand.)
Now a command to clear a northern ghetto
and Hoffmann's turn to read the orders
to proceed as usual.

But the captain has stomach pain and dysentery.
Often it's best to refrain from motion so instead
from his bed he fusses over small details.
His men soon notice he tends to fall
ill on the eve, bedridden
before the action.

With Hoffmann on sick leave Trapp
asks Berlin to relieve the captain of his command.
Moved to the front he'll win an Iron Cross, belie
his former comrades snide remarks and heal
his bruised pride. The spirit willing,
had the flesh refused?

Wohlauf

Vice-Commander Wohlauf, chief of the battalion's
First Company, an officer with belief in himself
And a lust for success that often came to grief.
Schooled in the regime, the SS by twenty-three,
recalled from duty in Norway for lack of restraint
and here at twenty-nine he's back in favour
as Trapp nurses his career but his men still see
a pretentious man, their showy 'Little Rommel.'.

This is a captain of romance. Due to marry
in June, out of the blue his battalion is sent
to Poland but Trapp will relent and he weds
but returns to command a company at Józefów.
Soon Wohlauf has his new spouse visit him.
A wartime honeymoon. His greatcoat draped
over his bride, she'll climb aboard his truck
alongside her captain on an August round-up.
The head of his convoy Wohlauf issues orders.
Hiwis already sotted are shooting so wildly
even his police take cover and everywhere
corpses as Jews make their way in thousands
to the market-place one hot late summer's day.
Those who faint are shot. Frau Wohlauf,
already four months gone, takes off her coat,
stands in her dress at the market looking on.

To a man his First Company now take offence
that a woman sees their violence. A trace of shame
as a horrified Trapp must face his officer down.
After the Serokomla massacre he and his bride
pass some days in Hamburg. The honeymooner
returns but stays only weeks as ill with jaundice
he seeks recall. His one brother has been killed
and his father just dead, as an only living son
his request is granted. Exit Captain Wohlauf.

Culmination

After massacres and cleared ghettos
a hunt for any fugitive disappeared
to live underground, daily outings
to hound absconders hid in forests
now tracked by faeces found in snow
or giveaway chimney pipes attract
stalkers to the prey. Farmers' stolen
crops betray their hungry presence.
A hunter drops a grenade in a bunker,
any survivors sprayed with gunfire.
A dozen or two at a time, entire
families perish as volunteers pursue
the chase. No duress just a tenacious
tracking down. Once again the face
to face of Józefów as Battalion
101 clock up another thousand.

Seniors withdrawn, others moved on
in the turnover and still the battalion
blooded at Józefów participates
in the Harvest Fest as inmates
of Lublin labour camps march
to zigzag graves. Speakers blare
music to mute and counterpart
gunshot and lined along the route
Reserve Battalion 101
sentinel a cortège to extinction,
the Germans' biggest single *Aktion*;
in three November days alone
forty-two thousand Jews slain –
half the battalion's whole campaign.
Such ordinary men now lend a hand
to kill some eighty-three thousand.

FIGURES

Shtiler, shtiler, lomir shvaygn,
Kvorim vaksn do.
S'hobn zey farflantst di sonim;
Grinen zey tsum blo.

Still, still let us be still.
Graves grow here.
Planted by the enemy,
they blossom to the sky.

Shmerke Kaczerginski
translated by David G. Roskies and Hillel Schwartz

Summons

Meditate that this came about. Imagine.
Pyjama ghosts tramp the shadow of a chimney.
Shorn and nameless. Desolation's mad machine
With endless counts and selections. *Try to see!*
For each who survived, every numbered
Arm that tries to hold the wedding guest,
A thousand urgent stories forever unheard;
In each testimony a thousand more suppressed.
A Polish horizon glows with stifled cries:
Who'll wake us from this infinite nightmare?
Out of the cone of Vesuvius their lives rise
To sky-write gaunt silences in the frozen air.
A summons to *try to look, to try to see.*
A muted dead demand their debt of memory.

Figures

After days and countries of a roughshod ride
Dishevelled children edgy and overstressed:
A boy scolded won't stick to his mother's side,
A miss who hugs her doll against her chest.
Boarding-school girls clamber from the train
In hats with blue ribbons trailing in the air,
Pleated skirts and socks straightened again
Five by five, holding hands and unaware.
A fifteen-year-old will recall how she loses
A mother who opts to leave her on her own,
A neighbour's child so forlorn that she chooses
The other side. A waif shouldn't vanish alone.
Figures forever sealed in a molten Pompeii,
Marrow spread as bone-dust in Polish clay.

Arrivals

Clamourings for water, even a handful of snow.
By day the glimpsed places, in the dozed night
Groans or bickering until their wagons slow
And crash open in a station's eerie floodlight.
Uncanny ordinariness. 'No Baggage', they're told.
A dozen SS men with a stony indifferent air
Move among the arrivals questioning 'How old?
'Healthy or ill?' and pointing either here or there.
Men won't abandon wives. 'Together afterward,'
They're reassured. Some mothers unreconciled
To leaving small children are soon transferred:
'Good,' they say, 'Good, just stay with the child.'
A finger is pointing. Caprices of fate allotted.
Frozen silence of lives unseamed and parted.

There

Non-stop. A sweated shift of *Sonderkommando*
Remove remaining traces of a previous batch
And hurriedly prepare the set for another show,
Another intake into this theatre of despatch.
A clothes-peg carefully numbered still forestalls
A final panic. Such a well-rehearsed scene
With signs hung on the changing room walls
To extol in several languages merits of hygiene.
A squalid journey and now the need to scour
Arrivals. *Remember your number*...unctuous
Reassuring speeches as spruce SS impresarios
Cozen and seal their victims into a shower.
Just affable ushers. No time wasted. No fuss.
In every heart one moment when it knows?

Here

After disinfection, broken oversized shoes,
Berets, blue stripes and the shaven head,
A large yellow Star of David for the Jews,
For criminals green triangles, politicos red.
Elaborate madhouse of rules and signs of caste
Beatings. Starvation. A *Kapo*'s whim and sway
Unravel reason. Here no future or no past.
Maybe the sap and cunning for another day.
A ladle of watery soup traded on the sly,
A broom filched, a shoe-patch, rations of bread.
Each for himself. Father steals from son.
Parched but denied an icicle Levi asks why?
There's no why here. Shorn and striped biped,
A tattooed number who'd once been someone.

Qui vive

Always on their wits. Day by day to postpone
The inevitable in a brutal catch-as-catch-can;
As months draw skin tighter over a cheekbone,
Steinlauf washes to remember he's still a man.
When to queue to arrive as the soup is thickest,
To sleep on a pillow of belongings, not to leave
Bowl or shoe untended. Survival of the quickest.
Ruses and dodges of endurance. Endless *qui vive*.
The submerged or exhausted slow beyond caring.
A week, at most a month. Then the *laissez-faire*
Of the overcome and a last ghostly indifference
To hunger, squalor, beatings or fear. Just staring
Listless and vacant goners. *Muselmänner.*
A light in their eye already shines their silence.

Threads

Three a.m. roll-call of skeleton labour.
Chin up, chest out until the *Kapo*'s gone;
Hands tucked under armpits of a neighbour
Huddling the glazed will to carry on.
Phantom bodies move outside their mind
As cold claws and ices deep in the marrow.
On the double! Various teams, assigned
A ditch to dig, sand and stones to barrow.
Weeks totted from when they first arrive,
Argued over, checked so someone could say
For certain if any of them manage to survive,
So and so died on such and such a day.
Just somebody to pass another's story on;
Tiny threads of time loop beyond oblivion.

Night

Night after night they sink in muds of dream:
There among their own in warm midsummer
They tell their story to friends who always seem
Distant, somehow unable to hear a homecomer.
Attuned to the sound, old hands wake but hold
Back and so are sure they'll arrive in between
Bucketfuls, never are sent half-clad in the cold
To empty warm urine into a frozen latrine.
They drift again towards a sleep that gnaws
And lures the mind with phantom food until
Many lick their lips or work their jaws;
Dreams both tempt and cheat the hungry will.
Short fitful hours when a Tantalus replays
In feverish stereo broken nightmares of days.

Ensemble

In summer by camp gates an ensemble's concerts:
As squads of inmates are filing past in fives,
On stools in their pleated navy-blue skirts
And lavender scarves they play for their lives.
Chosen by an exam, many who'd been *virtuose*
Now grind a music complicit and empty-eyed;
A band conductor from a famous Vienna café
Parodies for all she's worth her life outside.
Brisk marches to keep everything on the go.
In strict tempo marionettes in rags they slept in
Jerk their stiffened joints and swollen feet.
Then *The Blue Danube* or even *The Merry Widow*
For a commandant who loves waltzes. A violin
Is singing against the grain its hollow upbeat.

Ravens

They untangle, lug, stack and kindle the dead.
Chosen on the platform for brawn, broken in
Hell for leather, men clubbed and goaded
As still among the bodies they recognise kin.
Shirkers are shot. Others harden to endure
As stokers of hell, well-fed privileged caste
High on their pickings. A three-month tour
Of duty before they in their turn are gassed.
Sonderkommando, Levi's 'crematorium ravens'
Fallen beyond his compassion's greyest zone;
Soiled by fellow blood, vultures and cravens,
Cain sucking his marrow from Abel's bone.
Pity these ravens for what driven ravens do;
Bitter complicity that Jew should oven Jew.

Elite

Stars of the show they strut their daily stage:
Roll-call, undressing-room drama, the rite
And frisson of power, rivalry, bursts of rage,
Gratification of swaggering in this limelight.
'Caps off!' The slowest to remove their caps
Are plucked out in rows of five to undergo
A routine of physical jerks until they collapse,
And battered then to death by a block *Kapo*.
An elite trained by public shamings to comply
Now turn humiliation into ritual bloodshed.
Snappy and insouciant the SS cast an eye
Over the count to check the newly dead.
Thrilled by quivers of fear in lives they own,
They crunch paths gravelled with human bone.

Lily

Lab women and men in SS gardens consort.
Lily is engaged to a Pole in an undercover
Courtship. Her striped dress tight and short,
Lily is twenty and styles herself for her lover.
Never face on, their whispered rendezvous,
Cigarettes from a ration, cucumbers he thieves,
Small forbidden gifts and their billets-doux
Hidden for pick-up under a pumpkin's leaves.
Her fiancé sent to another commando, his friend
Fetches a note and is nabbed. A coded complot
In sweet nothings? Prepared to take the rap,
He's beaten but refuses to tell until in the end
The Pole owns up to save him. All three are shot.
We are, she'd written, *like plants so full of sap…*

Chinks

Here Jew, politico and gypsy, misfit and thief,
This underworld where push comes to shove
In a squad's *esprit de corps*, moments of relief,
First rough fellowship edging towards love.
Under the chimneys shows of gratuitous aid,
Things forgone, a gesture for a friend's sake:
Lulu offers a tea ration to a parched comrade,
At roll-call fainting neighbours slapped awake.
Wolf hums his repertoire while Levi advises
Bandi, innocent Hungarian, to steal to survive;
In the black of night Lorenzo the mason rises
To filch soup which keeps his protégés alive.
For some, for a while, bitter and sweet parallel
As rifts of light blink through the walls of hell.

Alone

Sprawled barracks, shacks, a conglomerate
Of *Kapos*, commandos, a shifting grey zone,
Clutches of friends, dices of time and fate
And each satellite camp a globe of its own.
Bunked head to feet in a jam-packed hut.
Polish. Hungarian. Greek. Every new arrival
Reshuffles the cards. Flux and through-put.
Bonds of language, a connivance of survival.
Each somewhere someone's remembered face.
At Buna, Monowitz, Auschwitz and Birkenau,
For most an unheard passing leaves no trace
But eking their starved wits a few somehow
Endure to witness through one memory's lens.
The silent alone fathom the depth of silence.

REFUSALS

Unter dayne vayse shtern
Shtrek tsu mir dayn vayse hant,
Mayne verter zaynen trern,
Viln ruen in dayn hant.

Beneath the whiteness of your stars,
Stretch out toward me your white hand;
All my words are turned to tears –
They long to rest within your hand.

Abraham Sutzkever
translated by Leonard Wolf

Spoors

Murmurs

Under black sunlight the will to endure;
A victim dares to overturn her soup bowl,
Warsaw's ghetto defended sewer by sewer,
Reckless White Rose of the siblings Scholl.

What to do if Germans evacuate Amsterdam?
Frank gossips to her diary in an annex room.
In Bürgerbräukeller Elser primes his bomb;
Wolski the gardener is hiding Ringelblum.

At Birkenau, Salmonovitch shins a flag mast.
'Nearly a hundred,' he replies when they ask
His age. Six hundred boys beaten and gassed.
A crematorium log buried in a thermos flask.

Crackles of resistance. Cussed moves to stall
The beast. Cards flung from trains, spoors
Of memory, whispers behind a gossamer wall.
Static of refusal. A grit of risk and gestures.

Blumenfrucht

Sosnowiec, June of '42 and Germans
in hospitals threw infant Jews from a window
to trucks below. The rest leave for Auschwitz.
Five youths somehow sought to thieve arms
from a German's quarters. Blumenfrucht caught,
he wants to shoot but an officer's dog sinks
teeth in his hand. Resolute as they set alight
wooden chips stuck underneath his fingernails;
even a two-day session on an iron net fails
to break him and when he screamed he said:
I will not speak, I am dead no matter what.
A mother brought to cajole him. Still he refuses.
Captors esteem such self-control but something
in his mettle unnerves the regime. By right a Jew
is swung in daylight, a warning to *Untermenschen.*
Blumenfrucht hanged before his morning broke.

To Life!

On the lookout, ready for any fate
Dabrowa Tarnowska's prayer-shawled
Rabbi Isaac would wait
With followers. Found and hauled

From their hide-out underground,
They're herded to a Jewish graveyard.
Someone unseen by their guard
Passes a vodka bottle around

And facing each waiting assassin
They drink their toast *lechayim!*
As linking hands they begin
To dance. At once mowed

Down. A preventable episode.
Enraged the squad cuts
Their bellies and tramples on them
To spill their mutinous guts.

Praise him with the timbrel and dance.

Hallowing

1

At Kelme, the ditch dug, Daniel
Rabbi asks a commandant's leave
To speak for a while to his people.
Alright speak but make it brief.

Unhurried in the face of the commandant:
The sanctification of the name, trace
And travail of a shadow-desiring servant,
No longer to act, simply to embrace.

Time to end – an officer butts in.
Willingly, lovingly to accept our fate.
The ditch graves gape and wait.
I have finished. You may begin.

2

Ringelblum beaten for nights on end
Refuses to name any gentile friend,
Asks: Can death be so hard to bear?
To deny their gloating over his despair.
A Warsaw bunker someone had betrayed
And all thirty-eight caught in the raid.
A switch of cell? Prisoners contrive
His rescue. Slim chance to stay alive.
And are his children doomed all the same?
So it's the way of Hallow-His-Name.
Kiddush Ha-Shem. Humble acceptance.
For many just the sign of their silence.

Recording

And will anyone ever know?
In Vilna they wanted, in case,
Someone outside the ghetto.
I'm the victim. I'm the witness –
A camp slogan. Defiance
Of record. Charged remembrance.

Birkenau's chronicler Lewental
Buries his thermos in the ash
Of crematorium III, journal
for a final revolt, a cache
Of testimony, resistance of word,
Troves of memory interred.

Four hundred pages of diary
In the minuscule hand of Etty
Hillesum, a crammed story
Of sudden ripening that forty
Years away will resurface.
Spoor of a life. A trace.

Survival

1

As smoke from burning wood the will
To survive leaves a ghosted heart;
Parents and sons of Olga Lengyel
Chambered, her husband once sighted
Through the wire, she tilts to the brink
Till drafted by camp resistance. A part
To play: intelligence link by link
Along a human chain the underground
Flits contraband, a parcelled explosive
Hazardous as the angle of a *Kapo*'s head.
At least to die for something beyond.
We lived to resist. We resisted to live.

2

Pell-mell nights in a parched cattle car,
Parted from loved ones into a bizarre
Seesaw of eerie calm and rampage
Of the *Kapos*' random virtuoso rage,
Broken by ghettoed months, too numb
With disbelief to adapt they succumb.
A few by grit or hazard can adjust.
Ruses of refusal. A shared crust.
Carmen's bartered pail for Delbo's
Drought. More than his soup, Lorenzo's
Resistance. A gesture of human rapport.
Levi's something still worth living for.

Just

Leopold the thief feeds his protégés,
tends their needs in his *pied-à-terre*,
a Lvov sewer. Laundry. Prayer books.
A year to liberty and ten survive.

Freelance, Albert the local masseur
bicycling Jersey to rub his clientele;
his fee in kind duck eggs and bread
secreted to his fosterlings underground.

After *Kristallnacht* Priest Lichtenberg
protested against transports to the East,
prayed for Jews and internees. Arrested
for his prayers, he dies en route to Dachau.

Austrian Anton Schmidt, the sergeant,
sought to flit Jews by army truck
to Białystok – still thought safe.
But caught, he too forfeits the light.

A Gruszka Zaporska unnamed tended
Six in his cowshed. Raided he's gunned
As he fled for his life. Gendarmes return
To wipe out wife, daughter and son.

To save just one is to save the world.
On bitter ground the wind-blown seed;
Lone random flowerings of courage.

Haunted

Dazed in a sudden comeback from oblivion
Displaced huddle into a surge of rebirth,
Children named after their ashen gone,
Firethorns lavishing berries on stony earth.
Swaying in a brittle future so many cling
To one another, pooling their orphan genes,
Their broken youth lived out in offspring,
Angels of their parents' interrupted teens.
Vulnerable vessels, survivor urge to protect.
Fragmentary disclosures. Eavesdrops. A tattoo.
We must be ready after what happened to us.
Children tabbed by anxiety. Always checked.
Stains of what happened seep slowly through.
Aroma of mistrust, distant fall-out of Vesuvius.

Deep in the memory gene a black sun.
History is over, be happy like anyone.
Would they help, give bread? Delbo
Asks every face. No assumed tomorrow.
Defiant normality. Success of reborn day
Almost holds nightmare moments at bay
As they make their lives. The busy scarred.
And yet to know not to drop your guard,
Never to count on another human being.
You're alone. Something always missing.
Undertones of grief lurk below a crust
Of everyday. Half-smile of broken trust.
Behind a flimsy partition ghost parents call,
Siblings eavesdrop behind a gossamer wall.
A doubleness only revenants understand.
Wounded alone know the wounded land.

Even the numbed and busy daylight cracks
A survivor's mask. A subconscious goblin
Triggers surreal *déjà vu*, flashbacks,
Replays, clusters of torments breaking in.
The dentist's drill smells of burning bone,
In a car behind a bus the choking fumes,

A crane's gibbet dangles inmates to atone
Escapes, a cinema queue for shower rooms.
Delicate balance between the dark and light:
Ordinary work-filled days with nervous rifts
Weigh against the nightmare's haunted realm;
Grown older, days again brim with hindsight,
A psyche lopsiding as its fragile poise shifts
And burdens of memory threaten to overwhelm.

Voices in the bowels of the ark cry out:
Hear us too! Cracked voices of drought
As from cattle cars hosanna faces stare.
Primo Levi now steps so softly into air.
Points thrown, a barbed unerring train,
A rifted trust never quite trusted again;
A keeper brother unkeeps Jean Améry,
Still red embers burning into memory.
Es mus azoy zayn. Who witnesses a witness?
Celan's burden of so much ash to bless,
Insomniac being, silent in the Undivided
He marks: *Sometimes his genius goes dead
And sinks into the bitter well of his heart.*
One by one by one our witnesses depart,
Softly the shaft, the orphan's satin despair
Over the parapet, down the well of a stair.

Against the odds unearthed diaries, fragments.
In milk cans and tin boxes Ringelblum's blow-
By-blow journals, sudden cache of documents
Dug up out of the ruins of the Warsaw ghetto.
Planting a tree some Polish children chance
On thermos-flasked notes of Zalmen Lewental,
The Greek Jew's slow-release resistance,
Birkenau *Sonderkommando*'s time capsule.
All fugitive chronicles sealed into airtight
Jars interred with rubble and sunk below
Rebuilt houses, lives still waiting on the light.
Write and record. That a world may yet know.
Dubnov's orders, *shtetlekh* and ghettos wiped
From the earth's face: *Schreibt un farschreibt.*

Cry the shibboleth in an alien land.
Trucks of half-skeletons, the demand
Of the rabbi's son, desolate Elihu:
Show your power. This is against you!
Nothing happens. No lightning rod.
Sonnenshein shouts *There's no god.*
Six million brothers Cain can kill.
Black sunshine. Ratchetings of evil
As chill winds blow across a bowl
Of stars. A world rattles on its pole.
Broken vessels of a god in hiding,
Agony's grinding down, a sliding
Back to sacred nothingness that hovers.
Beckonings, maybe. No more. A lover's
Invitation rumouring through the dark.
Rustles of absence in a silent ark.

Le Chambon

Hinge

Whipped by one of those skinflint winds
that blows in across such exposed tableland,
a thin dark-eyed woman shawled in snow

Picks her way to *rue de la Grande Fontaine*,
that led beyond its curve to a staid presbytery;
In Le Chambon, they said, someone might help.

Remote sanctuary, ice-skinned city of refuge,
tombstone grey, wind-bitter Huguenot village,
stubborn asylum on the granite Plateau du Velay

where Chazot the preacher once burnt at the stake
and Nantes' promise breached, a thousand or so
more Protestants had sought refuge and settled here.

Rocky ground, steady and fertile in its remembrance
of the centuries' outbursts, nest of unarmed resistance
sentried to the south and west by spent volcanoes.

Over the German border into northern France,
and now her final chance she has fled southward;
in Le Chambon, they said, someone might help.

Wind and snow whirl off the Lignon River.
A half-numb tap. Swinging on a hinge of memory
The door opens. '*Naturellement*, come in, come in.'

Divergence

Holidaymakers gone, the twin granite villages
Le Chambon-sur-Lignon and Le Mazet winter in.
Three months of yellow summer, nine of grey.

Curt streetscapes and stoic cut-stone homes,
bleak outskirt of somnolent farms and forest
where dissident Huguenots once hid their pulpit.

Two craggy villages paired in a single story,
four centuries of shared and broken ground,
the same prepared soil before this ordeal.

A deep resistance sways on its stealthy roots,
urgent offshoots of risk, a subterranean hum,
in a humus of quiet trust, Le Chambon burgeoned.

Everything aware and ajar. The secret room,
webs of messages and kitchen *savoir-faire*,
Teams of guides to dare the mountains by night.

Somehow bitterer winds now blow in Le Mazet
to chill the marrow. No apron of sensuous grain.
No scatterer. No sower. No Spring. No *grande fontaine*.

Against the stranger's need, Le Mazet's shut door.
A ground so harrowed though no seed is sown.
My neighbour is only my own. A narrowed love.

Pastor Trocmé

'Death, death, death,' his sigh on arrival,
'I'm entrusted with helping a tiny village die.'
Through the ashen stonewalls of a presbytery
deep slanted windows ration their sunlight
on a Basque style tablecloth. Yellow, red, black;
colours warm and volatile enliven a room.

Driven, turbulent Trocmé. A boy of fourteen
he'd seen a jawless German after the Somme.
An etched image. Or was it Kindler, born-again
telegrapher, refusing to bear arms at the front?
A flicker of sun-caught yellow in a cloth's design;
what must be done to save this village's soul?

Here the hungry depths of Huguenot memory.
Jews? But we only know one human kind.
Throwback of whispers among old outsiders
as Trocmé trudges in snow to far-flung farms.
Kitchen to kitchen. A tremolo of counteraction,
a calm obstinacy spreads its undertow of trust.

Still that temperament. Yellow, red and black
as doubts that will often plague his mind by night.
A few hundred or even thousands sheltered?
Too small a thing to do? And was it cowardice
to shun all force? Bitter chaffings of despair,
a blood-red desire to gun the Führer down.

No time for idle compassion. A violent man
bridled by love, Trocmé has begun to sow
in the long readied soil of grey Le Chambon
his stubborn mustard seed of quiet resistance.
A stranger's face caressed. A door ajar.
City of refuge, lest innocent blood be shed.

Impresario

Great summer clumps and bushes of wild broom
yellow and warm a desolate hinterland before
it greys back to a wasteland nine-month winter.

Even then the bony withered fingers of *le genêt*
warm again, yielding their acrid perfumes
to thaw the chill stony rooms of Le Chambon.

The pastor's wife is tending her kitchen stove
snapping and bending the broom's wizened branches,
She hears a numb tapping on the presbytery door.

It's the hunger she notices in the snow-haloed face,
a half-glance preparing to retrace her steps
through the entrance porch. 'Of course, come in!'

'Come in!' She bustles a stranger toward heat to hear
her news, fusses her to eat at their long wooden
table, her sodden shoes shoved in the oven to dry.

In a blizzard she crosses a square to the Town Hall.
'But no,' says the mayor, 'just run her out of here!
'Will you save one woman and destroy us all?'

No arguments. Madame Trocmé exits to snow,
reluctant impresario of an underground trust.
The first of hundreds lying low, secreted

in safe houses and farms near the pine forest,
over mountains out of harm's way to Switzerland.
A city of refuge. A hamlet for waif and stray.

But where else could they go? A Chambonais' shrug
Plays down the dangers. We had to take them in.
I couldn't close a door against a stranger's face.

Contagion

Out from the hub of Le Chambon's counterstand,
Slow spread and rub-off of their bedrock love.

In childbirth, Magda had nearly bled to her end.
As Trocmé watched by her bed in his dark heart

he knew he'd relished survival; even as she sank
his mind raced with plans, how he'd begin anew.

But shouldn't he yearn for two to meld into one?
A broken mystic so shocked at his self-concern.

Later she mends and he confesses his own dismay
at how his spirit could stray in a future without her.

'Oh never mind' – her bifocal nature that understood
those gradients of love and let-go always undefined.

Her earth-nearness countervails his earnest strain,
holding a tense balance in the scales of a passion.

His ardour still never sure where to draw the line;
perpetual apprentice in the yaw and pitch of things.

Two intense temperaments contrary and at one.
The nave of their resistance fanning outwards.

Risk

Besieged centuries of dissent and lying low
These still waters lodged in a spent crater,
a mountain people silent, cunning, secretive.

Something stirred. Swirls in a brackish pond
as word spreads of a summer round-up in Paris;
rumours of Jews massacred in the far east.

Stonily refusing to betray any broken stranger
Le Chambon's grey dissenter presbytery becomes
a hub and clearing house, an eddying centre.

In the temple they ask *Which now of these three,
thinkest thou, was neighbour to him that fell
among the thieves?* Somehow an interrogative mood

ripples and widens out across the community.
And about thirteen leaders, *les responsables*,
discuss and relay the same implacable question:

Who is my neighbour? The Gestapo tightens its grip
but a daring begins to outweigh every new risk;
the Chambonais already grown surer of their answer.

More and more fugitive children are housed.
Madame Eyraud's *pension* forever open door,
her fourteen or so boarders mothered and homed.

Then a pacifist school of makeshift classrooms,
An ease of welcome and deft rule bending
blending both refugee teachers and pupils in.

On the periphery houses with backdoors that open
onto woods where the hidden flee when the farm
dogs bark their alarm as a round-up approaches.

Sober Chambonais spontaneity that needs to move
less from above than outwards. An *esprit de corps*
quickens in the margins. Some centrifugal love.

Swift and decisive responses, no over-command,
almost as though they thrive on risks just taken;
this village alive in the jazz of its chosen danger.

Nameless

Maybe it comes from the garrison city of Le Puy.
A hasty call from a nervous employee
who somehow contrives to forestall Gestapo round-ups.
Those lives in his hands as he lifts a phone;
unknown amateur mole, his heart in his mouth.

The same warning from the same nameless voice.
Beware! Beware! Tomorrow morning!
No one knew from where the call had come.
But whoever it was, was always right,
just one night's notice given to raise the alarm.

All houses in Le Chambon and nearby combed.
Routine call for identity papers,
Machine-guns poised, doors hurriedly unlocked,
walls knocked for a hollow sound,
cupboards, attics, cellars but no Jew found.

Throughout the day invisible messengers flit
beyond the village, make their way
to warn the outposts of a coming daybreak raid.
Uprooted from another makeshift lair,
evacuees prepare to vanish into the forest.

At the core some anonymous urge to disobey.
His quick staccato communiqué issued
before the click on a swiftly recradled receiver:
Attention! Attention! Demain matin!
A furtive courage crackling down the line.

Trouble

Trocmé and two right-hand men are incarcerated.
First distrust, then respect for these Huguenot
Inmates, a camaraderie of spirit almost as though
Another Le Chambon grew as they met and debated.

Fragile city of trust, an innocent countermine
Far too dangerous to handle. The camp supremo
Ordains their release. And just before they go
An oath of allegiance two of them refuse to sign.

Back in the huts fellow internees are horror-struck:
Refuse to sign? A scrap of paper in a dossier?
You must be a skunk with skunks! Even Trocmé
That stubborn night would doubt the line they took.

'Pack your bags – we want no trouble in the compound,'
They're told next morning. Orders come from on high.
And no need to sign. They return to say goodbye.
Holding hands closest comrades gather around,

Sing *au revoir* to the tune of 'Auld Lang Syne'.
The Huguenots survive. *Only* au revoir *my brothers.*
Freighted to Polish camps or Silesia the others
End in the chambers or the maw of a salt-mine.

Misgivings

Years after Magda Trocmé will recall
and still regret that first bitter deceit
counterfeit cards made for a Monsieur Lévy.

Without a faked identity the man would die.
And yet to lie? A slide to the demimonde?
Once beyond Eden some candour forever lost.

These faked forms, papers forged or falsified,
Things denied, fudge and ruses of concealment,
Each silent half-truth went against the grain.

More a time for action than for contemplation
or an old temptation to keep our hands clean;
would we've been purer if we'd shut our door?

A shed innocence. Impure metal of humankind.
'Never mind,' she shrugs, 'What else could we do,
'Who could they turn to if the Chambonais balked?'

Le Forestier

1

'A lonely, young, sad and beautiful man'
This was how years afterwards the Chambonais
Recall him, brown-haired Dr Roger Le Forestier
Who settled in Le Chambon before the war began.

Villagers warm to boyish irresistible innocence,
Sober Chambonais drawn in by his spontaneity,
A strange, colourful figure who lives so vividly
His life seems much more real than his absence.

He falls for Danielle with all the swarm and whirl
Of a nature utterly guileless and open-hearted.
'A woman as handsome as himself,' they said
'How he couldn't stop being in love with the girl!'

From the outbreak eccentric surgeon to the Maquis
Patching up injured guerrillas until he'll refuse
The partisans his red-crossed ambulance for use
As a troop-carrier. Shunned, he blunders to Le Puy

To prove himself, trying to have two Maquisards
Released but underground passengers have played
Into Gestapo hands, Sancho Panza betrayed
By a gun they'd hid on the sly in the boot of his car.

He pleads his beliefs: *lest innocent blood be shed*
Chambonais had hidden Jews. His youthful candour
Moves Schmehling, Le Puy's garrison commander,
To free him if he goes to tend German wounded.

A chance to flee but his gratitude refuses to shirk.
Already Schmehling's acquittal has been subverted
By messages to Lyon the Gestapo have sent ahead,
They nab him as he sets off to Germany to work.

Later Danielle tracing her husband Le Forestier
Learns of a hundred and twenty murdered near Lyon,
Rummages sacks of their belongings. In the final one,
A button with the name of his tailor in Montpéllier.

2

A score years on the Trocmés visiting Munich
sought out Schmehling (now a retired schoolmaster
living in a bomb-damaged house) inquired of him
why those last grim months while they scoured
villages nearby and knew Le Chambon was a den
of resistance, why then did they desist from closing in?
'I believed,' he replied, Le Forestier had told the truth,
nothing in our violence could kill Chambonais dissent,
and I worked to delay the Tartar Legion's round-up.'
So why, the Trocmés press, was Le Forestier murdered?
'That Gestapo bastards should gull me! At night
I wake and that beautiful, beautiful woman is there
with her two small children begging me for their sake
to spare her husband. I see them as they take leave
of that man, her confidence in me that he would return.
What must she think of me?
                              1944,
August 20th, some days before the liberation
of Paris, a Gestapo squad ablaze with a night's
drinking had herded from Le Forestier's jail scores
of prisoners out to an abandoned farmstead where
they were gunned, stacked, doused, set alight,
their clothes packed into sacks. Neighbours had heard
the screams of those the bullets had failed to kill.

'What must she think of me? ' His eyes now fill
with tears. In a low voice André Trocmé replies:
she has not as yet been able to forgive you.
Voilà tout! The Trocmés leave him to his grief.

PRISONERS OF HOPE

הֲיֵשׁ בִּלְתְּךָ גּוֹאֵל, וּבִלְתִּי – אֲסִיר־תִּקְוָה ?

Is there any redeemer like you?
Or any prisoner of hope like me?

Judah Halevi
translated by Nicholas de Lange

Round-up

Whoever it was took this photograph

Zeros on a boy's eyes that want to grow
Bigger and bigger the more you gaze,
Deeper and deeper in the sideways
Sunlight asking us how we can know

The words to put in the mouth of another?

Dust-veil

1

Three millenniums and minds still rake over
Hekla's third post-glacial outbreak, uncover
ash interred under a thousand beds of ice
tephra that spreads to Uist and Shetland.
Had this dust-veil produced such changes,
not just immediate havoc but shifts of climate
ramifying right across a northern hemisphere?

Those years Ireland's oaks had narrowest rings
Norway's snowline fell and the Caspian rose;
even the Alpine winter now grows harsher,
the Danube overflows to flood the Hungarian plain.
Does the great Mycenaean reign end by drought,
famine rout the Hittites from the Anatolian plateau,
Hekla's outburst unsettling over half our globe?

2

Still in autumn harvest feast of Sukkoth.
A fugitive garden hutch, a fragile booth,

Lonely tabernacle, wilderness *pied-à-terre,*
Wandering other always at home elsewhere.

Is there any redeemer like you? Poet Halevi
Asked, *Or any prisoner of hope like me?*

Roaming three millenniums: Mesopotamia, Egypt
By the Nile, Babylon, Nineveh the same script

Of exile and bondage and wilderness sojourns
Crying towards Jerusalem. Caravan of returns.

The battered wife of a God she can't forsake,
Even an enemy's bruisings a lover's keepsake.

My love encamps where'er you pitch your tent...
And chastens the body your sweet blows have bent.

3

Liberator on the move, knife on the throat.
Thousands of lives herded westwards;
laggards, stragglers riddled and ditched.

We were not allowed to turn our heads
but we knew what the shooting meant.
Sometimes five hundred shot per day.

At Blechhammer marched into huts
to sleep, then torched. Burn or run
the gauntlet of sweeping gunfire.

On a cliff-top road beside Palmnicken
gunners mowed them five abreast
dead or alive into the freezing Baltic.

Rhyme nor reason. Knife on the throat
as a black sun sinks. The Reich
pared to its bare skeleton of hate.

4

After Liberation Socha the thief is struck
Down on a Lvov street by a passing truck;
Poles cross themselves as his juices ooze
In a gutter. *God's reward for aiding Jews.*
London's streets dance as war ceases;
In Poland still a rondo of hate's caprices.
Bełżec, Sobibór, Treblinka, Chełmno,
More than all the Auschwitz archipelago;
Treblinka, Chełmno, Bełżec, Sobibór
Of two million, a hundred and nine endure.
Testifying in Lublin one of Bełżec's two
Killed as he homes from court. Bastard Jew!
Five Auschwitz, Mauthausen and Buchenwald
Survivors the Polish Home Army halt
In a car near Nowy Targ stripped and slain.
An angry shadow falls on the face of Cain.
At Kielce eight-year-old Henryk Blaszczyk's
Pretended on July 4th of '46
That Jews had seized him for special rites.

A medieval rumour fanned now re-ignites
And forty-two are shot, axed or stoned.
More than half the survivors flee Poland.

5

Hierarchies of doubt among the blessed few.
Another man's wounds? Who slept with a *Kapo*
To cheat the hungry kiln or made it through
Dancing moonlight naked to pleasure Gestapo?
Hoarded brunt and guilt of unspoken years.
Business as before. Over and over nightmare
Of ghostly homecomings where no one hears.
To endure to tell the world but do they care?
Heels are taller and hem-lines lower again.
A glittering eye can't stay the wedding guest
Who shirks the bony hand of too much pain;
A world that lusts for life soon loses interest.
For years tattoos of memory travel incognito.
They didn't understand, they didn't want to know.

6

Slowly a cone has bled its anger,
red lava cools off and browns.
In Northeim Girmann's ousted enemy
comes back to run the City Hall.
A policeman in Battalion 101
peached by his ex-woman and sent
to Poland names a sergeant, lieutenant
and major under whose command
he'd shed blood of Jews and Poles.
The policeman and Trapp are executed.
Gnade fell in action but most fled
like Lieutenants Hoffmann and Wohlauf
to Hamburg as career policemen until
in '67 an assiduous investigator
will accuse them. An eight-year sentence
(four for Hoffmann on appeal) but the State
withdraws. The conviction rate too low.
Who understands or wants to know?

7

Ancient Mesopotamian spring fest
Woven by the scattered or oppressed
Into a sombre history of complots
To erase a people without trace.
Feast of Lots.

Mordecai, outsider who wouldn't bow
And refused to kowtow
To Haman, jumped up Amalekite
That plotted to destroy the Persian Jews
Out of spite.

Mordecai and niece Esther outsmart
Haman the palace upstart...
At Minsk in '42 at least
Five thousand from the ghetto killed
To mark their feast;

Thirty miles west of Lódź the Gestapo's
Readied gallows
And Jews made play hangmen
To their own ten sons to avenge
Haman's ten.

For the festive bread of deliverance
A stone of remembrance
With noosed ghosts in bas-relief;
Ashen calendar of bitter eruptions,
Almanac of grief.

8

No gain or purpose. Just gratuitous hate.
Never before? And yet we can't be sure?
Cinders raked over in the earth's grate
Peoples buried in ash that left no spoor?
Thousands of Aztec victims paraded yearly
In Tenochtitlán, taunted up the stairways
To the killing stones high above the city;
American natives wiped by *Conquistadores*.
Even among narrow-eyed cruelties a shudder.

Time and motion as two masked figures unclasp
A canister dropped in a sunken bunker's eye-hole.
Shift and breach of the known, an under-judder
As a volcano spits warnings through a fumarole.
Fall-outs of tephra still blow beyond our grasp.

9

'Ten days it rained ashes and the rains were grey',
a chronicler writes with dismay: bitter weather,
dry fogs, dimmed suns, blights and failed harvests,
signs from heaven as the Shang dynasty runs down.

A Chinese eyewitness to Hekla's Far East fall-out?
A spewing fireball spreads a dust-veil of desolation,
pall of travail, those broken and scattered peoples.
Destruction turns all their presence into absence

unless some testimony breaks their infinite silence.
In remembrance resides the secret of our redemption.
Out of this eruption, can we prepare another climate?

Sign

Lonely Yahweh breathes in
And out ten vertebrae of a human;
Another inhaling of love
But blown too hard to glove

Their bones and seven vessels
Explode into night, cells
Of a divine soul we bring
Back by deeds and prayering.

Talmudic riddles and lucid
Yiddish...joyously I stride
In Warsaw, Vilna or Lvov.
Other. Among and not of.

Unhomed. Smitten with eternities.
Thou shalt separate three cities...
Lest innocent blood be shed.
The milk and meat divided.

The wood, the fire and the lamb.
And I am tired as I am
A Jew, wading through blood.
I no longer have the hardihood...

Glatstein at fifty odd
Quarrels with a wounded God.
We, your radiant vessel,
Palpable sign of your miracle.

Is this what haters hate?
The chosen choosing to separate.
Kedushah. Apart and vagabond.
Singled out. Bearers of beyond.

Paradise

The sea is the sea. A chimney's just a chimney.
Bride kissed through a veil of wounded piety.

I love the birth of light, the pure fantastic
Of the naked and the real. Without bombastic.

Shalom, to be safe, to be healed and whole.
A wood of candles now the Wailing Wall.

Down a corridor of history the booted pogrom
Still echoes a broken rhyme with crematorium.

Black milk, black snow, black sun, black bloom.
Paradise pushes its way out of my tiny room.

Maybe a half eternity of God's restless time,
How often to trust to heal such broken rhyme

In Abraham's breast? *And all my yesterdays*
I sense among blossoms of blood-flecked lilac sprays.

Babel

A city, a tower whose top may reach to heaven.
Has would-be Babel fallen all over again?

So sure we'd been of plot and *mise-en-scène*,
A tick-tock dénouement, slow but certain.

Visions of control, primrose track to hell;
Stoked ovens, gaunt shadows of Babel.

Broken forever old spinning-jenny's thread,
Our long and trusted dream of progress dead.

Bitumen for mortar, they said, *brick for stone*.
Paths of Auschwitz paved with ash and bone.

Still trembling in our galaxy's outer spaces
The crying silence of six million faces.

Stretching

So is all history one secret narrative of power
Broken in the brick and rubble of Babel's tower?

Hard-bitten Atlas, our hands thrown in the air
Are we too disillusioned now to bother to care?

Our stories become labyrinths of irony that turn
On irony. Fiddlers fiddling while a world may burn.

He breaks me down on every side and I am gone
O you who stalked the barren road to Babylon

Or walked the desert as second Jerusalem fell
And Titus of Vesuvius shattered Herod's temple

Show us again some end to shape our storyline.
A feast of rich food and well-aged wine...

Isaiah's imagination stretches somehow to cope;
In Jeremiah's darkest scroll a jazz of hope

That stirs even in the deepest cries of silence:
Then shall the young women rejoice in the dance.

Glimpses

After a tough day selecting who'd live or die,
For light relief Mengele had the camp cellist
Anita Lasker play him Schumann's *Träumerei.*

But in concerts under Mahler's niece's baton
Hints of perfection outside a chimney's shadow.
Behind all hopelessness a kind of life went on.

Depths of survival. Klezmer or jazz or *céilí,*
A story squeezes at the edge clamours of music;
Out of darkest histories, profoundest gaiety.

A feast of rich food and well-aged wine.
Visions beyond loosening back into a world
Too deep and copious for black suns to shine.

Imagined surprises, surprises beyond our ken.
Dream and reality feeding circuitries of hope;
A promise to remember, a promise of never again.

Waking

Can how we remember shape what we become?
A criss-cross of testimonies in every medium.

Delbo says do not look in the eyes of the cellist,
A cellist recalls her music as a means to resist.

Walking ghosts in staccato clips of a newsreel;
Six million one face in the melancholy of a still.

Lucky Szymborska, *a hook, a beam, a brake;*
Celan's waking to *black milk of daybreak.*

Humble siftings, a patient tentative process;
Angles and tangents of vision, layered witness.

No closure. No Babel's towering overview;
With each fugitive testimony to begin anew.

Memory a frequent waking out of forgetfulness;
Dissonant cries of silence refuse to quiesce.

Imagine

More than ever seductions of Babel's tower.
New ways of control,
Accrued information, the software of power.

The overlords and barons of print and screen,
Oligarchies of news
Shaping our images. Everything overseen

By Argus whose hundred eyes never sleep:
Snooped bites of memory,
The bug and zoom to eavesdrop and peep.

A traffic camera that can zero in at will,
Constant vigil in the heavens,
Whereabouts triangled, tabbed by a mobile.

The benign are keeping a watch over us.
Imagine another black sun,
An all-knowing stony insomniac Argus?

As never before we promise never again.

Never

That any poem after Auschwitz is obscene?
Covenants of silence so broken between us
Can we still promise or trust what we mean?

Even in the dark of earth, seeds will swell.
All the interweavings and fullness of being,
Nothing less may insure against our hell.

A black sun only shines out of a vacuum.
Cold narrowings and idols of blood and soil.
And all the more now, we can't sing dumb!

A conversation so rich it knows it never arrives
Or forecloses; in a buzz and cross-ruff of polity
The restless subversive ragtime of what thrives.

Endless dialogues. The criss-cross of flourishings.
Again and over again our complex yes.
A raucous glory and the whole jazz of things.

The sudden riffs of surprise beyond our ken;
Out of control, a music's brimming let-go.
We feast to keep our promise of never again.

Repair

Never, never again. Pleading remembrance
Whispers through the gossamer wall:
Promise us at least this. An insisting silence.
We begin to repair, to overhaul

Soft habits of the psyche, trying to find
Fault lines, trembling earth-shelves,
The will overreaching limits of mind
Grounding worlds in private selves.

Wounds always ajar. In its aftershock
Our earth still trembles and strains.
Tentative moves. Even to probe a rock
Stratum, to map the fault planes?

White noise and quivers. Shifts of geology.
What might be salvaged? Hesitance
Of first mendings. Delicate *perhaps* or *maybe*
Tracing detours of repaired advance.

Faces

Neat millions of pairs of abandoned shoes
Creased with mute presence of those whose

Faces both stare and vanish. Which ghetto?
Warsaw, Vilna, Łódź, Riga, Kovno.

Eight hundred dark-eyed girls from Salonica
Bony and sag-breasted singing the *Hatikvah*

Tread the barefoot floor to a shower-room.
Friedländer, Berenstein, Menasche, Blum.

Each someone's fondled face. A named few.
Did they hold hands the moment they knew?

I'll change their shame to praise and renown in all
The earth... Always each face and shoeless footfall

A breathing memory behind the gossamer wall.

Soon

Soon now their testimony and history coalesce.
Last survivors fade and witnesses to witnesses

Broker their first-hand words. Distilled memory.
Slowly, we begin to reshape our shaping story.

A card from a train in Warsaw's suburb Praha:
We're going nobody knows where. Be well, Laja.

That someone would tell. Now our second-hand
Perspective, a narrative struggling to understand.

Victims, perpetrators, bystanders who'd known
Still cast questioning shadows across our own.

Some barbarous. Mostly inaction or indifference.
Hear, O Israel still weeps their revenant silence.

Abraham pleaded for the sake of the ten just.
Our promise to mend the earth? A healing trust?

Reprise

To remember to break the middle *matzah*
To lean to the left and taste again *maror,*

To pour salt-water on eggs at the Passover,
Share around the untouched cup of Elijah.

Risks. Fugues of detours. Spirals of reprise.
A feast of rich food and well-aged wine.

A light too broad for any black sun to shine.
Scope of conversations, brilliance of what is;

To love the range and fullness yet to recall.
Your golden hair, Margarete, your ashen hair...

Next year in Jerusalem! Parting toast and prayer.
And still they breathe behind a gossamer wall.

ACKNOWLEDGEMENTS

The Gossamer Wall is a distillation over several years of various aspects of the Shoah and it is hoped that it will encourage readers back to the primary sources, in particular to the first-hand accounts of witnesses in which the poems are grounded, but also to historical or scholarly studies and the imaginative literature which undergird them.

Among the numerous testimonies of survivors are Primo Levi's *If This Is A Man, The Truce, The Drowned and The Saved* and *Moments Of Reprieve*; Charlotte Delbo's *Auschwitz and After*, Elie Wiesel's *All Rivers Run to the Sea*, Etty Hillesum's *An Interrupted Life*, Anne Frank's *The Diary of a Young Girl*, Jacques Lusseyran's *And there was light* and Anita Lasker-Wallfisch's *Inherit the Truth*.

Some of the historical works which the poems draw on are Sir Martin Gilbert's *The Holocaust*, William Sheridan Allen's *The Nazi Seizure of Power*, Christopher R. Browning's *Ordinary Men* and Philip Hallie's *Lest Innocent Blood Be Shed*, along with many other studies such as Ron Rosenbaum's *Explaining Hitler*, Christopher R. Browning's *The Path to Genocide*, J.P. Stern's *Hitler*, Joachim Fest's *Plotting Hitler's Death*, and Aaron Hass's *The Aftermath*.

Other books which the poems point to are Richard L. Rubenstein and John K. Roth's *Approaches to Auschwitz*, Inga Clendinnen's *Reading the Holocaust*, Edith Wyschogrod's *An Ethics of Remembering; Contending with Hitler*, edited by David Clay Large, and *In and Out of the Ghetto*, edited by R. Po-Chia Hsia and Hartmut Lehmann.

The imaginative literature dealing with the theme includes Anne Michaels' *Fugitive Pieces* (from which the title is taken), Elie Wiesel's *Night*, David G. Roskies's *The Literature of Destruction* (which provided several epigraphs), *A Treasury of Yiddish Poetry*, edited by Irving Howe and Eliezer Greenberg, and John Felstiner's *Paul Celan* and *Selected Poems and Prose of Paul Celan*.

I'm grateful to Dr Elizabeth Maxwell for inviting me to read from these poems as part of the international conference *Remembering for the Future: The Holocaust in an Age of Genocide* at Oxford where I had crucial conversations with survivors, scholars and those who teach and hand on the history of the Shoah to another generation.

I'm deeply appreciative of the advice and support of my friend Professor Peter Ochs, as well as Dr Margie Tolstoy, Dr Nicholas De Lange, Professor Gila Ramras-Rauch, Dr Wendy Whitworth, Dr Guy Beiner, Angela Gaw and Dr Margaret Gowan. I'm also grateful to David Arnold, Paulette Goldstein, Batsheva Dagan and Oren Baruch

Stier for their interest. I'm especially thankful to friends Vigdis and Erik Bjørhovde, Marie Rooney, Dermod Dwyer, Helen O'Sullivan, Robert Kruger, Hallgrímur Magnússon, Ken O'Brien, Valerie Hannigan, Audrey and Walter Pfeil, Daniel and Perrin Hardy, Deborah and David Ford (for his constant encouragement and counsel) and, above all, to Bríd.

Acknowledgements are also due to the editors of the following publications in which some of these poems first appeared: *The Harp, The Patterson Review, Remembering for the Future: The Holocaust in an Age of Genocide*, ed. John K. Roth and Elizabeth Maxwell (Palgrave, 2001) and *Third Way*.